basics of biblical parenting

three principles that will transform your family

paul ch

Copyright © 2006 by Striving Together Publications.
All Scripture quotations are taken
from the King James Version.

First published in 2006 by Striving Together Publications, a
ministry of Lancaster Baptist Church, Lancaster, CA 93535.
Striving Together Publications is committed to providing tried,
trusted, and proven books that will further equip local
churches to carry out the Great Commission.
Your comments and suggestions are valued.

All rights reserved. No part of this book may be reproduced,
stored in a retrieval system, or transmitted in any form or
by any means—electronic, mechanical, photocopy,
recording, or otherwise—without written permission of the
publisher, except for brief quotations in printed reviews.

Striving Together Publications
4020 E. Lancaster Blvd.
Lancaster, CA 93535
800.201.7748

Edited by Cary Schmidt and Maggie Ruhl
Cover design by Jeremy Lofgren
Layout by Craig Parker

ISBN 1-59894-015-5

Printed in the United States of America

Table of Contents

Introduction

Training to become a commercial airline pilot is no easy undertaking. In addition to hundreds of hours of classroom training and private study, commercial pilots are required to log at least 250 hours of flight time and pass an intense examination by FAA personnel. Thousands of hours of training, reading, studying, memorizing, and flying are required before a commercial pilot is legally given responsibility for even one passenger.

As parents, how long did you study, how many classes did you take, and how thoroughly did you prepare before you were given legal responsibility for your child? Rearing a child is a far more difficult and weighty responsibility than flying an airplane, yet "parenting licenses" are easy to come by in today's society—no tests to pass, no books to read, no examiner to make sure you're ready.

Consider how different the American family would be if every parent was required to invest 250 hours of training before the arrival of their first child! How much more effective would you be if you had to *earn* a "parenting license"? How much more prepared would you be to train, guide, and lead a young family if you took *your* responsibility as seriously as a commercial airline pilot takes *his*?

President George Bush, Sr. was recently interviewed regarding his concerns for our nation. During the interview, questions were asked about the tragedies in Iraq, our relationship with Russia, and other world issues. Cutting through all of the global politics, in a moment of truthful perception, President Bush replied, "America's greatest national danger is the disintegration of the family."

His statement is true. The American family is disintegrating before our very eyes, and the average family has no idea how to reverse the downward trend—even in their own homes, let alone on a national level. Our families are falling apart, and America sees it but has no idea what to do about it. The average family accepts *less than mediocre* as normal. We accept fighting, anger, bitterness, and conflict as "normal family life." We accept rage and hatred as "common to every home." In the process, we're missing the great joy and wonderful experiences of "being a family."

Perhaps you can identify. Do you ever find yourself long on problems and short on answers when it comes to leading and nurturing your family? Do you find that your relationships at home are virtually non-existent or strained at best? Do you feel as though you missed "parenting school" and you've been dropped into the seat of a 747 headed for a crash landing? If you can relate—if you know that your family has big needs—then keep reading! There's hope just ahead!

God understands. His plan for the family remains intact, and He is waiting to help implement His principles to bring your family back to health. While the world is at a loss for how to create and lead a healthy family, God's blueprint and original design still work!

What if you could cut through all the secular, experimental thought on "family life" and find out the truth? What if you could heal your home, enjoy your children, and recover strong relationships by applying basic, easy-to-understand principles? Most importantly, what if you could partner side by side with the original Designer of the family? What if you could take the seat of "co-pilot," and allow God Himself to guide your children and your family into a safe landing?

Friend, you can land your family on the truth of God's Word and rely on His proven principles to grow and guide a loving, joyful, and blessed home. You don't have to "experiment" with the unproven and failing popular philosophies of the day. You don't have to crash-land your family. He is waiting to help you, and this book was written to show you how. You don't have to endure 250 hours of flight training to be a good parent! God can prepare you much more effectively. With Him, you have a supernatural advantage against this monumental problem.

If your family is in the midst of disintegrating, God's grace can put it back together. If your family is doing "fairly well" by your standards, God desires to "take it to the next level"! No matter the needs, God's

Word has the answers, and God's Holy Spirit will empower and enable you to apply those answers to your own family. Through Him, you can learn expert parenting skills and experience the happy family life you always dreamed of enjoying.

In the coming pages, we will explore three foundational, biblical principles that, if applied faithfully, will radically transform and heal your home. Think about that—just three principles with the authority of Almighty God behind them! They work because He designed them to! They work because He blesses them.

God didn't create the family to disintegrate or to crash-land. He designed it to fly successfully. He desires for you to enjoy your family life and to love your children and your spouse. He designed your home to be a wonderful place of love, laughter, and happiness. He is the Author of a good thing of which America has completely lost touch.

William Bennett, who formerly served as Secretary of Education, rightly stated, "The unmet needs of our children is as compelling as an attack from foreign enemies." What are these unmet needs? Why is America losing so much ground in family life? I believe three foundational needs have been all but forgotten, and these three overarching truths can make the difference.

They sure beat 250 hours of flight training, and they are a lot less painful than a crash-landing!

Let's find out more about them.

CHAPTER ONE

Children Need Balanced Restraint

In 1 Samuel 3:13, God chooses a very unique word in reference to Eli's failure as a father. He says of Eli and his sons, *"He restrained them not."* The Bible word *restrained* literally means "to rebuke, to make weak, or to discourage a certain type of behavior." The Bible is saying that Eli did not properly discipline his sons. He did not intervene in their lives with balanced, biblical restraint. He left them to themselves and allowed them to defile both themselves and others. The Bible bears out this principle in Proverbs 29:15, *"The rod and reproof give wisdom: but a child left to himself bringeth his mother to shame."*

Most parents in today's culture are lost when it comes to properly restraining their children. Restraint in the average American household usually takes on one of two damaging extremes. Either it is absent completely, leaving children to themselves and their own devices, or it is harsh, angry, and overbearing, leaving children wounded and rejected. The first produces a lawless, self-centered individual who grows up thinking the world revolves around him. The second produces a wounded spirit and an alienated relationship, leading to bitterness, anger, and eventually destruction.

We need a revival of biblical restraint in our families—balanced restraint.

In the first few chapters of the book of 1 Samuel, God gives us an amazing contrast between two families—one family with balanced restraint and the other without. The first family, Elkanah and Hannah, exhibited balanced restraint, and God blessed it. Here is their story:

> *Now there was a certain man of Ramathaimzophim, of mount Ephraim, and his name was Elkanah, the son of Jeroham, the son of Elihu, the son of Tohu, the son of Zuph, an Ephrathite: And he had two wives; the name of the one was Hannah, and the name of*

the other Peninnah: and Peninnah had children, but Hannah had no children. And this man went up out of his city yearly to worship and to sacrifice unto the LORD of hosts in Shiloh. And the two sons of Eli, Hophni and Phinehas, the priests of the LORD, were there. And when the time was that Elkanah offered, he gave to Peninnah his wife, and to all her sons and her daughters, portions: But unto Hannah he gave a worthy portion; for he loved Hannah: but the LORD had shut up her womb. And her adversary also provoked her sore, for to make her fret, because the LORD had shut up her womb. And as he did so year by year, when she went up to the house of the LORD, so she provoked her; therefore she wept, and did not eat. Then said Elkanah her husband to her, Hannah, why weepest thou? and why eatest thou not? and why is thy heart grieved? am not I better to thee than ten sons? So Hannah rose up after they had eaten in Shiloh, and after they had drunk. Now Eli the priest sat upon a seat by a post of the temple of the LORD. And she was in bitterness of soul, and prayed unto the LORD, and wept sore. And she vowed a vow, and said, O LORD of hosts, if thou wilt indeed look on the affliction of thine handmaid, and remember me, and not forget thine handmaid, but wilt give unto thine handmaid a man child, then I will give him unto the LORD all the days of his life, and there shall no razor come upon his head. And it came to pass, as she continued praying before the LORD, that Eli marked her mouth. Now Hannah, she spake in her heart; only her lips moved, but her voice was not heard: therefore Eli thought she had been drunken. And Eli said unto her, How long wilt thou be drunken? put away thy wine from thee. And Hannah answered and said, No, my lord, I am a woman of a sorrowful spirit: I have drunk neither wine nor strong drink, but have poured out my soul before the LORD. Count not thine handmaid for a daughter of Belial: for out of the abundance of my complaint and grief have I spoken hitherto. Then Eli answered and said, Go in peace: and the God of Israel grant thee thy petition that thou hast asked of him. And she said, Let thine handmaid find grace in thy sight. So the woman went her way, and did eat, and her countenance was no more sad. And they rose up in the morning early, and worshipped before the LORD, and returned, and came to their house to Ramah: and Elkanah knew Hannah his wife; and the LORD remembered her. Wherefore it came to pass, when the time was come about after Hannah had conceived, that she bare a son, and called his name Samuel, saying, Because I have asked him of the LORD. And the man Elkanah, and all his house, went up to offer unto the LORD the yearly sacrifice, and his vow. But Hannah went

not up; for she said unto her husband, I will not go up until the child be weaned, and then I will bring him, that he may appear before the LORD, and there abide for ever. And Elkanah her husband said unto her, Do what seemeth thee good; tarry until thou have weaned him; only the LORD establish his word. So the woman abode, and gave her son suck until she weaned him. And when she had weaned him, she took him up with her, with three bullocks, and one ephah of flour, and a bottle of wine, and brought him unto the house of the LORD in Shiloh: and the child was young. And they slew a bullock, and brought the child to Eli. And she said, Oh my lord, as thy soul liveth, my lord, I am the woman that stood by thee here, praying unto the LORD. For this child I prayed; and the LORD hath given me my petition which I asked of him: Therefore also I have lent him to the LORD; as long as he liveth he shall be lent to the LORD. And he worshipped the LORD there.
—1 Samuel 1:1–28

In this story, Elkanah and Hannah incorporated balanced restraint in rearing the son God gave to them. They provided healthy, biblical control in their home. Hannah was a godly mother who was willing to expend herself for the nurture and admonition of her son.

Looking at Samuel's childhood, we see that Hannah's method of parenting was not complex. Though she had no previous experience, she trusted the principles of God's Word. She knew her parenting responsibilities were far beyond her, and she fully depended upon the help of God.

The *result* always bears proof to the success of the *method*. In Samuel's life, we see that balanced restraint was pleasing to the Lord because he was greatly used by God. Samuel was chosen by God to be the earliest prophet after Moses and was later listed as a spiritual leader in Hebrews 11. He was known as a minister of God who finished his race.

So, what exactly is "balanced restraint"? How does this principle play out in our homes? What does it look like? A closer look at Hannah's life reveals four ways in which she exercised balanced restraint as a parent. (I think you're going to be surprised by what true, balanced restraint looks like in biblical terms.)

First, Hannah promised Samuel to God.

Hannah stepped out in faith and gave her son to God, knowing she would not withdraw her vow. She recognized that her child was a gift from God and that he belonged to Him.

Hannah gave God first place in her life and fully committed her children to the Lord. First Samuel 1:11 says, *"And she vowed a vow, and said, O LORD of hosts, if thou wilt indeed look on the affliction of thine handmaid, and remember me, and not forget thine handmaid, but wilt give unto thine handmaid a man child, then I will give him unto the LORD all the days of his life, and there shall no razor come upon his head."*

You might wonder, "What does this have to do with restraint?" It's quite simple—everything! This attitude of submission toward God is where balanced restraint begins. The entire basis for a balanced, restraining relationship in the home is the love and fear of God—first in the parent and then transferred to the child. God must be the foundation of our homes, and as parents, we must recognize that we are under His authority. He is our God, and our children are gifts from Him. Parenting is all about Him, for Him, and because of Him.

Hannah practiced this principle of surrender. She placed herself under the authority of God and committed her own life and the life of her child to the Lord. She parented with pure motives to please God.

She restrained and nurtured her son, not for herself but for the Lord.

Have you done the same? Are you parenting out of selfish impulse or out of love and submission to God? Your children know the difference. When you parent selfishly with no regard or fear for God, you are driven by the whims of the flesh rather than the guidance of the Holy Spirit of God. Your temper, your anger, your cutting words are all indications of a spirit that is not yielded to God and a parenting philosophy that is not based on surrender.

You see, restraint at home begins with restraining your own heart as a parent. It begins with modeling a life of obedience to God. Why did Samuel grow to become an obedient young man? Was it simply because his mother was good at controlling him? No. It was because his mother was good at modeling balanced restraint in her own life. She recognized that she was the *"handmaid"* of the Lord.

If you're reading this book for a "quick fix" in your parenting skills, you won't find one. True transformation in the home begins with inspecting your heart before God. Are you living and modeling a life of balanced restraint to your own Heavenly Father? Are you following His commands? Are you obeying His Word? Are you honoring Him? If not, then you must begin right here! You cannot teach obedience or expect to properly restrain your child if you cannot be obedient to your own Heavenly Father. Unrestrained children do not produce restrained children. Your children are watching you, and they will mimic your relationships—especially your relationship with your Father.

Hannah was an obedient child before her Heavenly Father. It only stands to reason that she produced an obedient child in her home. If you are eager to get your family back on track, then I challenge you to follow Hannah's example. Submit and commit yourself and your child to God. Give God first place in your heart and in your home. Seek His control in your life and in the life of your child.

Balanced restraint begins with putting God in His rightful place in your heart and in your home.

Second, Hannah nurtured Samuel.

Based upon her vow, Hannah was only given a short amount of time to instill biblical principles into her son's life. Her wisdom and her diligence as a mother allowed her to prepare Samuel *"that he may appear before the LORD."*

Hannah's Choice

Hannah made a critical choice as a young mother to give of herself to her son and to prepare him for his future. When other pressures called her away, when other opportunities arose, she chose her son and his needs first. This was both honoring to the Lord and critical to Samuel's preparation for God.

First Samuel 1:22–24 says, *"But Hannah went not up; for she said unto her husband, I will not go up until the child be weaned, and then I will bring him, that he may appear before the LORD, and there abide for ever. And Elkanah her husband said unto her, Do what seemeth thee good; tarry until thou have weaned him; only the LORD establish his word. So the woman abode, and gave her son suck until she weaned him. And when she had weaned him, she took him up with her, with three bullocks, and one ephah of flour, and a bottle of wine, and brought him unto the house of the LORD in Shiloh: and the child was young."*

In Hannah's home, balanced restraint involved preparing her son for the service of the Lord. She took personal responsibility for training him. God's Word teaches this principle in Ephesians 6:4, *"And, ye fathers, provoke not your children to wrath: but bring them up in the nurture and admonition of the Lord."* We are commanded to raise our children in the truth of the Lord. Again in Deuteronomy 6:7 God says, *"And thou shalt teach them diligently unto thy children, and shalt talk of them when thou sittest in thine house, and when thou walkest by the way, and when thou liest down, and when thou risest up."*

Throughout Scripture, God instructs parents to take personal responsibility for the nurturing and training of their children. Beyond that, He commands us to diligently teach His precepts to our children while they are young. Bear in mind that Hannah could have used a number of excuses for "not being the right kind of parent." She could have argued that her husband had divided love with his second wife—a situation that was not pleasing to the Lord. She could have reasoned that she was new at parenting and didn't know what to do. She could have resented the fact that God had left her barren for so long, yet none of these things hindered Hannah from doing what God wanted her to do.

Hannah accepted her responsibility to train her son in the ways of the Lord and to prepare him for God's purpose for his life.

Our Choice Today

Frankly, we live in a culture where this kind of parenting is not popular. In the average American home, the school and the daycare do more in rearing our children than we do as parents. In the typical Christian home, parents reason that the Christian school and the youth group can do the job. We live in a day when biblical training is absent from the home. We have neglected our duty and relegated our responsibilities to others. Even as you're reading, you may be thinking, "Me? Teach the Bible to my children? I couldn't do that!"

Perhaps you feel ill-equipped. Maybe the thought is intimidating to you. Perhaps you, like Hannah, could think of a dozen reasons why you are too busy or unprepared for such a task. If that's the case, you may as well put this book down and carry on with life as you know it! Nothing will change. Until you begin transferring God's principles from your heart to your child's heart, you will not see lasting change.

Yet, if you would be like Hannah—unprepared, but willing—God could empower you and enable you to carry out this great responsibility. It may mean completely rearranging your life's priorities. It may mean simply opening the Bible in the evening rather than turning on the television. It will certainly mean making immediate changes and personal sacrifices to give your children more time and more deliberate Bible teaching and training.

Balanced restraint is a by-product of biblical principles. You cannot orchestrate true biblical order in a child's life apart from biblical instruction. Any attempt at restraint apart from a biblical foundation will be superficial and short-lived. Only God's Word and God's Spirit can take restraint deep into the heart of a child and establish it with grace. Hebrews 13:9 says, *"...For it is a good thing that the heart be established with grace...."*

Come back to God's original plan. Be the parent God commands you to be. Follow Hannah's example and give your children biblical nurture, no matter what age they are. It is never too late to begin, but the sooner you do, the sooner you will see balanced restraint develop in your home.

Third, Hannah sacrificed to God.

This one may catch you by surprise, but stay with me. First Samuel 1:25 says, *"And they slew a bullock, and brought the child to Eli."* Elkanah and Hannah exemplified a fully committed relationship with God through personal sacrifice. This was a powerful, unspoken lesson to young Samuel. His parents made God their first priority. They came to His house, worshipped Him from their hearts, and gave Him their best.

This family was a God-centered family and it was evident in their practice of sacrificial worship to God. Their love for God was evident in their "church attendance" and in their giving unto the Lord.

Now, you might wonder again, "What does this have to do with restraint?" Once again, it comes back to modeling a selfless life. Restraint in your home is really about teaching a young person to live for God and for others. Restraint is about selflessness. It is about putting God first and living a life of honor and sacrifice to Him.

Samuel's earliest memories were of his parents honoring the Lord in their lifestyle, not just their words. His earliest recollections were of his parents giving the Lord their very best offering. He learned in that picture a very important principle—our lives are to be lived in selfless sacrifice and honor to our Heavenly Father.

How Sacrificial Worship Impacts Our Children

I believe this pattern has two "paybacks" when it comes to establishing restraint. First, it directly teaches selflessness and service to the child. Samuel learned that serving God and sacrificing to the Lord was a high priority in life. Second, and more indirectly, God honors those who honor Him. In other words, God supernaturally intervenes in an imperfect family that is sincerely making an effort to honor Him. This is the less tangible, yet more important perspective on parenting. More than anything, we need God to touch our children with His blessing, and there is no greater way to invite that blessing than by honoring God and sacrificing to Him. He said these words later in this story, *"…them that honour me I will honour, and they that despise me shall be lightly esteemed"* (1 Samuel 2:30).

Friend, if you desire to establish balanced restraint in your home, exhibit a life of sacrificial service to God. Make church attendance a fixed commitment in your life. Make your tithes and offerings to God your first financial commitment, and let your children know it. Give your time and talents to serving God in your local church, and take your children on the journey with you. Involve them in serving others. Involve them in giving to God. Involve them in honoring God with you. I'm not talking about neglecting them for the sake of the ministry. I'm talking about serving God together!

Elkanah and Hannah reared Samuel in a home where God had first priority. As a result, Samuel grew up with balanced restraint, biblical structure, and a godly foundation.

God Honors Those Who Honor Him

Frankly, if church attendance is an *option* for you, so long as there's nothing better to do, then it will be impossible to truly establish balanced restraint. If God is somewhere between bowling and little league on your priority list, you're modeling the wrong life. If you're more interested in advancing your career or enjoying your hobby than you are in serving your God, restraint will be hard to come by in your home.

Over the years, I have seen many families who love and sacrifice for the work of God. I've seen many who serve God together. They embrace Him as God and live to honor Him and sacrifice to Him. In return, balanced restraint enters their home. Relationships are healthy where God's Spirit is welcome. Remember, God honors those who honor Him.

Fourth, Hannah honored God's people.

This is a very interesting character trait that we see in Hannah's life. You see, Hannah had a good reason not to honor God's man.

Look at what the Bible says in 1 Samuel 1:12–16, *"And it came to pass, as she continued praying before the LORD, that Eli marked her mouth. Now Hannah, she spake in her heart; only her lips moved, but her voice was not heard: therefore Eli thought she had been drunken. And Eli said unto her, How long wilt thou be drunken? put away thy wine from thee. And Hannah answered and said, No, my lord, I am a woman of a sorrowful spirit: I have drunk neither wine nor strong drink, but have poured out my soul before the LORD. Count not thine handmaid for a daughter of Belial: for out of the abundance of my complaint and grief have I spoken hitherto."*

Hannah's Response to Offense

This godly lady was simply pouring her heart out in sorrow to God, when the man who was supposed to be supporting her in that effort literally accused her of being drunk!

Hannah had a good reason to be offended by Eli the priest. It would have been easy for her to harbor bitterness in her heart toward him. She could have justified having a bad attitude, leaving angry, and starting gossip about Eli. Yet, had she done these things, her son would not have become the man of God he grew to be. It has been said, "A spiritual Christian writes his benefits in marble and his injuries in dust."

Hannah's reaction to these types of situations had an effect on Samuel's upbringing. She kept a right spirit toward God's man. She honored him as unto the Lord. Had she withdrawn from her God-given authority, she would have given Samuel a reason to do the same. Had she become angry and vindictive, she would have been turning the heart of her son away from the very man with whom he would serve the Lord.

Our Response to Offense

Have you ever disagreed with your pastor? Have you ever vented at home about a church requirement you did not fully understand? Have you ever had a disagreement or disappointment with a fellow believer? For most of us, the answer is "yes." During these moments of offense that come into all of our lives, we have a choice. We can follow Hannah's example and keep a right spirit, or we can allow Satan to drive a nail of bitterness into the foundation of our family. Either way, we will see the results in our children. If we guard our hearts and honor God's people, our children will learn to do the same. They will learn restraint. Yet, if we vent our anger and fail to restrain our irritation, our children will fail to restrain theirs. Hence, unrestraint again filters into our children's lives through our example.

By now, you may have noticed that the process of biblical restraint has much to do with the parents and little to do with the children. I knew you would be surprised! As parents, *we* need to decide to commit our family to the Lord. *We* need to train our children in their most formative years. *We* need to sacrifice our best to God, and *we* need to honor God and His authority structure even when we cannot see the

19

whole picture. By following these four wonderful character traits in Hannah's life, we can establish a family that is based upon a philosophy of balanced restraint.

God's Response to an Unrestrained Family

I hate to end this chapter on a negative note, but before we move on to our second principle, notice our other option. What happens if we fail to establish this biblical restraint in our homes? Let's go back to the story of Eli. It's a mess, so buckle your seat belt.

To make a long story short, Eli's sons were horrific problems for the people of God. The Bible details their sins and wickedness in 1 Samuel 2. God calls them "sons of Belial"—literally, sons of the devil. They were profaning God, committing immorality in God's house, and greatly dishonoring God and His truth. To make matters worse, Eli knew about their sin and did nothing. Short of condoning it, he simply did not restrain them. When these adult sons should have been "taken out back for a good beating," their father winked at their wrongdoing and did not prevent them from dishonoring God.

Later in a direct revelation, the Lord revealed to Samuel what He would do in response to Eli's inaction. He said in chapter 3:11–13, *"And the LORD said to Samuel, Behold, I will do a thing in Israel, at which both the ears of every one that heareth it shall tingle. In that day I will perform against Eli all things which I have spoken concerning his house: when I begin, I will also make an end. For I have told him that I will judge his house for ever for the iniquity which he knoweth; because his sons made themselves vile, and he restrained them not."*

When Eli should have been fighting for his sons, he did nothing. His silence was agreement. His lack of intervention was synonymous with "I don't care."

Strangely, somehow in American culture this inaction has been redefined as "patient love." Our reasons for not intervening and for not restraining are many: "He will grow out of it." "It's just a phase." "Everyone will sow their wild oats." "Boys will be boys." "Girls just wanna have fun." These are our popular "shrug off bad behavior" phrases. This is our way of laughing it off—of neglecting our God-given responsibility to intervene, to restrain.

How can we buy into this way of thinking? It doesn't add up. Leaving our children to themselves is always a recipe for disaster.

Think of it this way: If my son wanted to touch a burning stove, I would not stand back and watch him do it. I would not sit on the sidelines and hope he makes the right decision. I would not turn my back and pretend I did not see him. I would *intervene*! I would protect my child from hurt. I would *restrain* him! As parents, we must choose to intervene on the behalf of our children.

Renewing Balanced Restraint in Our Homes

Eli ignored his responsibility as a parent, and God judged him. If we do the same, God will judge us. God has called upon us to first model and then establish balanced, biblical restraints in our families. It is His will that we guide, guard, and direct the paths of our children.

Perhaps you're thinking, "If I did that—if I set up rules and guidelines and expected my child to follow them, I would lose them completely." Friend, that's faulty thinking. Sure, rules without love—restraint without balance—will produce rebellion, but that's where the word *balance* comes in. Restraint must be balanced with love and tenderness.

Strictness will not ruin your child but harshness will. Loving strictness expresses true compassion. Unrestrained harshness merely inflicts hurt. The two are very different, and it is vital that you discern between them. God does not call you to angry authoritarianism. He does call you to loving discipline and nurturing relationships. God's Word says in Proverbs 29:17, *"Correct thy son, and he shall give thee rest; yea, he shall give delight unto thy soul."* Delight comes from balanced, biblical correction; misery comes from lack of correction, as shown in the lives of Eli and his sons.

I received a letter about fifteen years ago that shows the effects of no biblical restraint.

Dear Pastor Chappell,

I feel a little odd writing to you, it just seemed important to contact you. I've no pastor here to talk to. I think it would be difficult to talk to anyone anyways. I am now in my first year of college. I feel more confused and uneducated now than I ever have in my life. I feel myself growing cynical, bitter, and critical with every passing day. I do not want to be like this, but I can't seem to change it…my mother and father have become extremely critical and embittered. It has now washed down over the children. I don't know why, I just don't feel like going to church. I'm so confused and angry.

When I was younger I was probably more concerned with church and with my Bible than I am now. I just don't know why, I just don't feel like going. Recently, someone gave me a Bible and I almost cried. My first thought was, what am I supposed to do with this? I've never even opened it since I received it. I set it down next to my old Bible and I've never opened it. My old Bible was torn and worn with dog-eared pages and now the new one is shiny and dusty.

One day maybe I'll go to church. I don't know why I'm unloading all this on you, but I do feel better. I think it's because you and the church had an important part in my earlier life.

When I read about a mother and a father who became extremely bitter and critical and a child who said it "washed down over the children," I felt compelled to beg parents to keep a tender heart toward God, toward their children, and toward God's authority in their lives.

Why is the American family disintegrating? Why are parents at such a loss, and why are children growing up with such confusion and frustration? Why has the "unhappy American family" become the "norm"? First, we have turned away balanced restraint.

What needs are going unmet in our children's lives? Children cry out for balanced restraint. They yearn for loving relationships that provide guidelines, discipline, and heart-felt nurture.

I have never met anyone who dreamed of becoming a drunk or living a life of mediocrity. Everyone desires to be above average, to make something of their lives. Every parent desires to rear children who will succeed in life. This can only be done if balanced restraint is implemented in the home. Restraint is the product of parents who honor the Lord and lead their children to do the same. Restraint is the product of parents who lovingly intervene with biblical guidelines and loving relationships.

Eli failed to restrain, and his sons were proof of this. The result was God's judgment.

Hannah succeeded in restraint—she modeled godly restraint. The result was God's blessing in a life that became great for God.

Friend, whether or not you feel prepared to parent this way, choose to do so! Choose to show forth a life wholly yielded to God, and lead your children on that same path. You see, biblical, balanced restraint honors God. It pleases and delights Him. God is on your side in this battle, and He will enable you by His grace to follow this principle. He will greatly honor you as you honor Him.

Who do you want your children to be more like? Samuel or the "sons of Belial"? We had better come back to balanced restraint before the future gets really messy!

CHAPTER TWO

Children Need Biblical Resources

On September 6, 1941, journalist Clarke Beach wrote the following words: "A Japanese attack on Hawaii is regarded as the most unlikely thing in the world, with one chance in a million of being successful. Besides having more powerful defenses than any other post under the American flag, it is protected by distance."

In one sense, he was right. The island of Oahu was equipped with the most advanced defense technology of the day. Pearl Harbor was equipped with a massive arsenal that would have easily conquered any expected attack. Yet, this reporter could not have been more wrong, as history verifies.

The Japanese attack on Pearl Harbor, just a few months after these words were penned, was one of the saddest days in American history.

As the first wave of 183 Japanese planes approached the island of Oahu, they were detected by a new radar system that was only operating for training purposes. Moments later, they were disregarded as American planes coming in from California. As this first wave of planes launched the attack, a second wave of 167 planes and a fleet of Japanese submarines followed—unleashing bullets, bombs, and torpedoes on our most powerful naval fleet.

When the two-hour attack was complete, twenty-one battleships had been sunk, and many others were severely damaged. Nearly 350 American planes had been either destroyed or damaged. Over 2,400 people were killed and nearly 1,200 were wounded. It was a devastating blow that could have been avoided.

Think about this. The world's most advanced radar system revealed early on that hundreds of planes were approaching Pearl Harbor. The world's most powerful battleships were available. Hundreds of American warplanes were stationed nearby. Thousands of battle-ready soldiers and sailors were present. All of the modern resources we could have possibly desired were at hand, yet the enemy caught us in a moment when our resources were not ready. The right tools were not being used properly.

I often see this same scenario played out in Christian homes. Satan is constantly on the assault. He is engaging us daily in a battle for our children. He desires to destroy them, and he is subtle in his strategy. It is sad that his attacks are often a surprise to Christian parents. They should not be. We have all the equipment, all the truth, and all the weaponry we need to uncover and defeat his attacks. Too often, we are caught sleeping or disregarding God's warnings and God's resources.

As Christian parents, we make the same mistake that American officers made on Oahu that dreadful day. We surround our families with the right equipment—a good church home, a family Bible on the coffee table, a Christian school, and a good youth group. Yet, this equipment does them no good if they are not trained to utilize it personally. Being surrounded with the right weapons is no guarantee that we will win the war.

Winning the war for our children is about having the right biblical resources, but it is also about using them effectively. It is a two-fold priority. As we discover what these resources are, please know that having them in your home is only half of the battle. You must move beyond "having the right resources." You must *use* them! You must teach your children how to do the same.

The Right Resources

God has not left you alone on this parenting journey! To the contrary, He has prepared the world's most advanced arsenal of parenting resources which stand at your disposal. They are foolproof because they come from God Himself. They are truth because God cannot lie. They are powerful because God is powerful.

Simply put, to win the war for your children, you will desperately need these biblical resources. You will need God's radar system to sense when and how the enemy is attacking your home. You will need God's defenses to protect your children from spiritual harm, and you will need God's arsenal to launch a counter attack.

What resources have you been depending upon to this point in your parenting journey? Perhaps you've been trusting your own wisdom or looking to secular philosophy. Anything less than God's biblical resources will leave you unprepared against your enemy. It is vital that you fill your heart and your home with God's "secret weapons" for spiritual battle. It is even more vital that you learn to use these weapons with skill.

What are these powerful resources?

The Word of God
Prayer
The Local Church

In the coming pages, we will take a closer look at each of these resources and learn how to use them in our homes. Once again, we will turn our attention more to you, the parent, than to the child. You see, for your children to use these resources effectively, you're going to have to teach them.

So, welcome to basic training. Let's get started!

Resource #1—The Word of God

The single most important resource for family life is the Bible. More than education, more than memories, more than cultural sensitivity, your children need to know and understand the Word of God.

In 2 Timothy 3:15 Paul said of Timothy, *"And that from a child thou hast known the holy scriptures."* Again in 2 Timothy 3:14 he referred to Timothy's training, *"But continue thou in the things which thou hast learned and hast been assured of, knowing of whom thou hast learned them."*

From a child, Timothy heard the instruction of the Word of God through his mother and his grandmother. He was taught to have an *"unfeigned"* faith—a sincere faith founded on Bible principles.

Proverbs 4:1–4 teaches us, *"Hear, ye children, the instruction of a father, and attend to know understanding. For I give you good doctrine, forsake ye not my law. For I was my father's son, tender and only beloved in the sight of my mother. He taught me also, and said unto me, Let thine heart retain my words: keep my commandments, and live."*

Parents are commanded to give biblical instruction in the home. Your child's core beliefs will be developed through this parental training and teaching. Don't wait until you believe they are old enough to understand. Teach them early, and let God begin to mold their hearts with His truth while they are very young.

Someone recently asked me, "How do you have family devotions with a three-year-old?" I told them, "Very briefly." It is not always easy to get the concept across to a young child. They might not always understand or comprehend the biblical principle being taught, but they will remember an open Bible and loving parents giving instruction.

The Bible says in Proverbs 23:22–24, *"Hearken unto thy father that begat thee, and despise not thy mother when she is old. Buy the truth, and sell it not; also wisdom, and instruction, and understanding. The father of the righteous shall greatly rejoice: and he that begetteth a wise child shall have joy of him."*

Overcoming Excuses and Awkwardness

Some parents think children are too young to comprehend God's Word. Others believe that children cannot understand the terminology used in the Bible. Yet, the Bible squelches this reasoning with one statement: *"And that from a child thou hast known the holy scriptures."* Children have the capacity to know God's Word; parents have the responsibility to teach God's Word. It's that simple.

In Deuteronomy 6:5–7 God says, *"And thou shalt love the LORD thy God with all thine heart, and with all thy soul, and with all thy might. And these words, which I command thee this day, shall be in thine heart: And thou shalt teach them diligently unto thy children, and shalt talk of them when thou sittest in thine house, and when thou walkest by the way, and when thou liest down, and when thou risest up."*

The *Merriam-Webster Dictionary* defines the word *diligent* as a "steady, earnest, and energetic effort." In this passage, God commands us to engage in the earnest and energetic effort of teaching biblical principles to our children.

Proverbs 4:1–4 says, *"Hear ye children, the instruction of a father, and attend to know understanding. For I give you good doctrine, forsake ye not my law. For I was my father's son, tender and only beloved in the sight of my mother. He taught me also, and said unto me, Let thine heart retain my words: keep my commandments and live."*

This verse shows the generational impact of a father teaching a son, who in turn teaches *his* son! These dads were serious about their mentoring responsibility. They taught their sons and gave them "good doctrine."

Can I be transparent with you for a moment? As a parent of teenagers, sometimes it is awkward for me to energetically pull up a chair and say, "How are you doing with God?" "Here is a verse I want you to know about." "Have you read your Bible today?" Sometimes this is uncomfortable for them and for me. I'm not saying this is easy. I am saying it is important—so important that it must overcome the feeling of awkwardness! Let's face it, it's much easier to just turn on the television, put on a movie, or let the kids sit endlessly before the PlayStation. Intentionally teaching biblical truth takes effort and persistence, but the rewards are huge! Maybe you can claim that Nike phrase as your own when it comes to teaching the Bible—"Just do it!"

There isn't a good excuse for failing to teach your children the Word of God. I pray you will accept God's command personally and give yourself to consistently training your family from this life-changing resource.

Making the Bible Practical

An *Associated Press* story recorded the death of a man who knew too much Bible for his own good. The headline read, "Alabama Man Killed in Bible Verse Contest." The story recounts, "A man who lost an early morning Bible quoting contest killed the man who beat him. A preacher's brother and the suspect were comparing their Bible knowledge outside an apartment complex each quoting different versions of the same passage. Police said the suspect retrieved his Bible and realized he was wrong. He said 'Taylor *did* know more,' and that's what made him mad. The man threatened Taylor saying, 'I'll kill you before the night is out' and left with two other people who had witnessed the exchange."

The man knew the Bible, but he certainly wasn't living it! God's challenge to parents regarding the Bible is that we teach our children how to *live* it. It's not enough that our children know about God or know *about* His words. They must see a living, practical application of those words. Proverbs 4:4 shows that this is a matter of the heart, *"Let thine heart retain my words."* God wants our children to understand and practice these truths from their hearts.

One of the greatest tragedies I see in fundamental churches is that people know the Bible, but they do not know God. They know good doctrine in their minds, but they do not know the God of that doctrine in their hearts! They have the appearance of godliness on the outside, but the heart is far from God.

Your children will study your heart more than they will listen to your words. If those words flow from a double-minded heart—a heart that is drifting from God—your words will be empty. Yet, if your godly words come from a truly godly heart—a heart that loves and honors God—those words will be powerful indeed!

Making the Bible more than a rule book is a heart matter. As parents, we must strive to instruct with our lives as much as we do with our words. Our words will make the Bible understandable, but our lives will make the Bible practical. Our children will listen to our instruction, but they will watch our application and emulate what they see.

How To Use Resource #1 in Your Home

Let me give you some basic ideas for putting this resource to use in your own home. How can you teach and apply the Word of God?

1. **Have family devotions together.** As a parent, call a halt to the day, open one chapter, and read God's Word together. As you do, ask God to give you wisdom in explaining and applying what you're

reading. If you pick a passage of Scripture that you're struggling with, pick another one. It's hard to go wrong. Proverbs and Psalms always have much to draw from. Pick a good Bible story. Let God guide you, and be creative.

2. Memorize a verse together. Pick one verse and make a game of it while sitting at the dinner table. Explain the verse and think of life situations when it applies. Teach your children what it means.

3. Talk about recent messages you've heard at church. A good family topic of discussion is a recent preaching or teaching message. Ask the kids what they learned in Sunday school. Tell them what you learned in church. Explain how God is working in your life.

4. Look for scriptural applications in everyday circumstances. Ask the Holy Spirit to guide you, and you'll be amazed at how "everyday occurrences" can become wonderful teaching moments of Bible principles.

5. Fill your home with good spiritual music. One of the best ways to learn Bible principles is through music. The right Christ-honoring music will do much to teach your children the ways of God.

6. Read the Bible by yourself. It's a good thing for your children to see you reading God's Word. Your time with God will speak volumes to them about how important God's Word is to your life. Also, the truths you learn in those private times can be taken to the next family devotion or meal time for discussion.

7. **Ask intuitive questions.** Accusation hardens the will, but questions stimulate the conscience. Consider which of these two statements is more stimulating to the heart. "I have not seen you reading your Bible lately," or "What did you learn in your Bible reading?"

8. **Communicate openly about spiritual things.** If you feel awkward about this kind of family life, it's probably because it is new to you. I challenge you to break through that barrier and let spiritual conversation and application become a normal way of life in your home. In time, it will just become a way of life, and it will be comfortable and natural for your entire family.

The Bible is God's supernatural resource for your home! It's wonderful if your children receive it at church and school, but they must receive it from you first. You can't afford to let this resource go untapped in your home. Knowing and applying the Bible must become a high parental priority right now.

Resource #2—Prayer

The second biblical resource that God gives to every Christian home is prayer. Prayer involves getting the attention of our Creator and entering into His presence with our burdens. Why is prayer important in parenting? Simply put, your relationship with God affects God's relationship with your children.

Prayer brings all of God's power and might you need in the fight for your family. Prayer invites God's presence into your home. Prayer impacts family life in a way that nothing else can.

This second great resource must be applied two ways. First, we must pray *for* our children. Second, we must pray *with* our children.

Prayer for Our Children

I like feeling that I have some control over the direction of my family, but I must be transparent with you again. As my kids have become teenagers and young adults, I have become more and more aware that I cannot be with them every second of every day. The older our children become, the less practical control we have on their lives. Frankly, that feeling is somewhat nerve-racking for a concerned parent. In our hearts, we long to protect and guide them, but in reality, we know that we cannot offer the omnipresent, omnipotent protection only God can give them.

Beyond that, if you have parented for very long, you can easily identify with feeling inadequate and unprepared, much like Hannah in our previous chapter. Hundreds of times I have found that my own wisdom and understanding of a situation falls far short. Hundreds of times I have "hit a wall" and wondered where to go next.

Friend, it is for these reasons and many more that we must consistently fall before God in prayer for our children. The magnitude of our responsibility combined with the subtlety of our enemy should drive us to God in prayer. We need Him! We need His intervention and His divine touch upon our homes. We need Him to do what only He can do.

The good news is that He is only one prayer's breath away, and He is eager to hear and respond to your sincere prayer as a parent. If you are wondering, "Where do I start with all of this information?" This is where! Pray. God specializes in helping those who call out to Him.

I encourage you to pray daily and specifically for your children. I pray daily for my children by name.

I pray that God will protect them, grow them in His grace, and guide them into His will. I pray that they will remain pure and that God would provide for them and sustain them.

> *Again I say unto you, that if two of you shall agree on earth as touching any thing that they shall ask, it shall be done for them of my Father which is in heaven.*—MATTHEW 18:19

God is moved to action when Christians pray together, whether they be parents or just two Christian friends. Mom and Dad, I challenge you to bind together in prayer for your children.

Susannah Wesley spent one hour each day praying for her seventeen children. In addition, she took each child aside for a full hour every week to discuss spiritual matters. No wonder two of her sons, Charles and John, were used of God to bring spiritual renewal to all of England and much of America. Susannah Wesley's commitment was to teach her children to pray as soon as they could speak.

When my dear grandmother passed away, I traveled to Chicago to be with my mom. While there, I took the time to walk around my Grandmother Brennan's house in Oak Lawn, Illinois. As I began to relive some cherished memories, I glanced at the pictures displayed on the walls. My family's picture was hung alongside many others, and as I paused there, my aunt came to me and said, "Paul, your grandmother never walked by here without stopping to pray for you."

As I look back on my spiritual heritage, I thank God for parents and grandparents who prayed faithfully for me. I know the blessings of God in my life are directly related to those prayers. The same will be true of your child—God's blessings upon their future will be directly tied to your prayers for them.

How easy it is when our children are struggling to point the finger of blame at the church, the school, or the youth group. Rather than point the finger of blame, bend the knee in prayer.

A prayer written by Douglas MacArthur to his son was found. He could not always be with his son due to war, but he realized the impact prayer made. He took advantage of God's presence.

A Father's Prayer
Build me a son, O Lord, who will be strong enough to know when he is weak, and brave enough to face himself when he is afraid; one

who will be proud and unbending in honest defeat, and humble and gentle in victory.

Build me a son whose wishes will not take the place of deeds; a son who will know Thee—and that to know himself is the foundation stone of knowledge.

Lead him, I pray, not in the path of ease and comfort, but under the stress and spur of difficulties and challenge. Here let him learn to stand up in the storm; here let him learn compassion for those who fail.

Build me a son whose heart will be clear, whose goal will be high; a son who will master himself before he seeks to master other men; one who will reach into the future, yet never forget the past.

And after all these things are his, add, I pray, enough of a sense of humor, so that he may always be serious, yet never take himself too seriously. Give him humility, so that he may always remember the simplicity of true greatness, the open mind of true wisdom, and the meekness of true strength.

—Douglas MacArthur

You have a "parenting hot-line" twenty-four hours a day directly to God. It is called prayer.

Furthermore, you have a God who is ready to intervene and to help you right now.

Prayer with Our Children

This second aspect of prayer is about transferring your heart relationship with God to the heart of your child, and it is perhaps the single most important thing you can do as a parent. In fact, it is so significant that the moment you commit to doing it, the devil will immediately begin preventing you. Satan does not want you praying with your child. He is powerless against this weapon, so be prepared for his attempts to keep you from it.

Make focused prayer with your child a daily habit. Focused prayer is more than a mealtime blessing. It is one-on-one, unrushed, and heartfelt. It is not an "autopilot prayer" but rather is sincere and unrehearsed.

I know many parents who fight frequently with their children but never pray with them. They are fighting the battle in all the wrong ways, and everybody loses. Regardless of how verbally "savvy" your teenager is, he will not be able to argue with your prayers. Regardless of how smart-mouthed your daughter can be, her tone will be silenced against your prayer on her behalf. Walls that no argument, no shouting match, and no standoff can break down, will literally melt against the echoes of your praying voice.

It's time for you to begin praying with your child. No matter where you are on this journey, no matter their age or spiritual condition, pray every day with them out loud. You will feel awkward at first. You will find many distractions to prevent you. But, if you will commit to this one activity consistently, you will see immediate spiritual progress that nothing else can produce.

Here are some suggestions for using this wonderful resource effectively with your child.

1. Pick a time or two every day when you will pray together. For many, this is in the morning before school and then again at bedtime. Your schedule may not allow this, and you may have to be creative but just do it.

2. Be prepared for resistance. First, Satan will resist you. You will be tired; something very captivating will be on the news, or a thousand other things will try to prevent you. Parents, work together as a team to remind each other. Second, your child may not want to pray with you. Pray anyway—out loud, with him listening. Your child can resist you, but he cannot resist your prayer.

3. **Start right away.** Whether your child is an infant or an eighteen-year-old, start now. You have no time to lose. If you wait for the right time, you'll miss your opportunity. Now is the right time.

4. **Find a quiet place and speak openly to God.** If you are thankful for your child, say so. If you are proud of your child, say so. If you are burdened for your child, say so. Speak freely and passionately to God on behalf of your son or daughter. Your words to God on their behalf will never leave their memory.

5. **Encourage your children to pray.** Teach them how to pray. Help them pray. If they refuse, give God time to break through their cold hearts with your prayers. In time, your son or daughter will open up and agree to pray with you.

6. **Don't quit.** Over time, this practice will become comfortable and natural in your family life. Your children will eventually anticipate it, and they will grow to greatly appreciate it.

7. **Make prayer spontaneous.** Surprise your family by talking to God when they least expect it. Acknowledge His presence while you're driving to school, on family vacation, or when you're just

sitting around the house. Again, at first you might feel strange doing this, but in time, your children will realize God is always with you!

We cannot over-emphasize the power and the privilege of this wonderful resource—prayer. The Almighty God of the universe invites you into His presence every day, and He allows you to bring your children! I hope you will accept His invitation, starting today!

Resource #3—The Church

The third most valuable biblical resource is the local church. Ephesians 5 teaches us that Jesus loved the church so much that He gave His life for it! Concerning church attendance, Hebrews 10:25 says, *"Not forsaking the assembling of ourselves together, as the manner of some is; but exhorting one another: and so much the more, as ye see the day approaching."*

Let me state it bluntly. God's institution for reaching the world, growing Christians, and preparing us for eternity is the local church. If Jesus died for it, then I think He would want us to be a part of it!

There is much to be said about the church, especially in a day when so many are "anti-church." Even popular Christian thought is purporting that the church has failed and that Christians would be better off in "home-worship" settings or worshipping God in our own ways. While I recognize that many churches are failing, I do not view that failure as a product of a flawed institution as much as a flawed philosophy of ministry. In recent years, many churches have become so much like the world that they have lost their distinctiveness and their effectiveness.

Yet, God's definition of the local church and His biblical instruction for how a church should function still stands! The local churches that Jesus died to establish are still alive and well, and they remain as an invaluable biblical resource for families today!

Friend, your family needs a strong, Bible-believing local church. Every Christian needs to meet with a vibrant, growing body of believers where the Word of God is taught powerfully and practically and where the work of God is being carried out biblically. Jesus Christ died to make the local church available to you, and He commands you to find your place in it and serve Him there faithfully. The local church is His gift to you and should be a place where you can bring up your children in the nurture and admonition of the Lord.

What Kind of Church?

With all the various types of "churches" that abound today, which one is for you and your family? I urge you to enter into this search asking God to guide you and help you understand the difference between truth and error. A true, Bible-believing church will have the following characteristics:

　　1. Bible authority—Choose a church that believes the Bible and only the Bible. God's Word should be the final authority for all matters of faith and practice in the Christian life.

　　2. Bible preaching and teaching—Choose a church that clearly and powerfully teaches and preaches the truth of the Word of God. Many churches today are presenting more pop-psychology than Bible truth. Find one that preaches the Bible and stands on the fundamental doctrines of the Word of God.

　　3. The preeminence of Christ—Choose a church that answers to Jesus Christ and that worships Him preeminently. He is the head of the church.

4. Christ-honoring music—Choose a church where the music is distinctly Christian and not similar to the world's pop-style music.

5. Grace-centered growth philosophy—Choose a church that teaches that the Christian life is motivated and guided by God's grace from within.

6. Grace-driven standards of holiness—Choose a church that will help you understand that grace teaches us to deny ungodliness. The right church will help you grow into Christ-likeness and will love and accept you on every step of your journey.

7. Biblical philosophy of outreach—Choose a church that is aggressively and courageously sharing the faith of Jesus Christ with others. Choose a place where your children will learn how to witness and win others to Christ.

8. A dynamic family spirit—Choose a church where God's Holy Spirit is obviously at work in the hearts of people.

9. Imperfect people with pure hearts—Choose a church where imperfect people make room for other imperfect people like you to become more like Jesus Christ.

10. So much the more—Choose a church that is doing more and more for the cause of Christ, not less and less. Many churches are dropping biblical convictions, shortening services, and cutting ministry. This is exactly opposite of what the Word of God means when it says in Hebrews 10:25, *"so much the more as ye see the day approaching."* Find a church that still has a Sunday night service, midweek Bible study, weekly outreach, and many more opportunities for you to grow in God's grace.

What the Right Church Will Provide for Your Home

Why is this resource so important? What will the right church provide for your home?

First, it will provide the Word of God. Your family will grow in God's grace through classes, services, revivals, and special meetings. Over the years, the right church will provide a strong, biblical foundation for your entire family and will help you weave that first resource of God's Word into the fabric of your home life.

Second, it will provide the family of God. We'll talk more about this in our next section, but suffice it to say, your family will greatly benefit from Christian friends, pastors, and spiritual mentors that you will find in a dynamic, loving church body. In Acts 2, the new Christians at Jerusalem continued in "fellowship" with the church. This simply means their friendships were established through the local church. The church became the hub of their social life. Don't let a few sad stories about hypocritical Christians or pastors who have fallen from ministry discourage you from finding a healthy local church.

Third, it will provide biblical authority. Placing your family in a Bible-believing local church brings your family within God's ordained, spiritual authority structure. He has ordained His church as His institution for spiritual change on this earth. To put it simply, you're fighting a losing battle with your kids if you circumvent God's structure of authority. God intends the right local church to play a big role in helping your family to grow in His grace.

What a wonderful resource—the local church! Take your children to the house of God. Introduce them to the family of God. Worship with them in a place that teaches and preaches the Word of God. Let them grow up with this resource that Jesus died to provide.

In many ways, these three resources—the Word of God, prayer, and the local church—work together. Without all three of them, your home and family life will be incomplete. God has given these three powerful resources as our weapons against an invisible enemy who hates our families.

Would you take a moment and recommit yourself to these three "secret weapons"? Remember, it isn't enough to simply know about them. You must use them!

CHAPTER THREE

Children Need Benevolent Relationships

Michael Anderson grew up in a Bible-believing, church in Spokane, Washington. From his boyhood, he loved the subject of space exploration and spent much of his time following the space program as well as watching science fiction television shows like "Lost in Space" and "Star Trek." He knew from an early age that he would become an astronaut. As he watched the first landing on the moon, he knew one day he would be among those who explored space. He said in his own words, "I can't remember ever thinking that I couldn't do it...I never had any serious doubt about it. It was just a matter of when."

For Michael, that "when" came in 1998, when he made his first space flight on the space shuttle *Endeavor*. The eight-day mission took him on a journey of 3.6 million miles that orbited the Earth 138 times. The mission was a dream come true with hundreds of memorable moments for the first-time space traveler.

Michael's second trip to space began on January 16, 2003, aboard the space shuttle *Columbia*. This sixteen-day mission conducted over eighty experiments, with the crew working long hours under demanding conditions.

On February 1, 2003, space shuttle *Columbia* was re-entering the earth's atmosphere when a breach in the outer shell of the craft allowed super-heated atmospheric gas to enter the body of the shuttle. In a matter of moments, flight systems began warning the crew that something had gone terribly wrong. Moments later, unable to withstand the intense heat, the space shuttle *Columbia* literally disintegrated in the Texas sky just sixteen minutes before landing. Michael Anderson and his six crew mates perished in the tragedy.

Just a few days later, President Bush shared these words with the American people as he reflected upon the life of Michael Anderson: "He also told his minister, 'If this thing doesn't come out right, don't worry about me, I'm just going on higher.'"

A few days before the mission, Michael said these words to his church family on video: "If I ended up at the end of my life having been an astronaut but having sacrificed my family along the way or living my life in a way that didn't glorify God, then I would look back with regret; having become an astronaut would not really have mattered all that much."

Although his mission turned fatal and his life was lost through tragedy, Michael Anderson's children will have a memory of a dad who knew what really mattered in life. He knew that he was saved by the grace of God, and he knew that his family relationships took priority over his personal desires and life's work. He was a man who understood that life is more than dreams and paychecks. He made a deliberate choice as a husband and father to keep his family first as he navigated his life choices.

We have seen that the American family is disintegrating for the lack of balanced restraint and the lack of biblical resources. Now, let's turn our attention to this third and final mission-critical need—benevolent relationships. Just as Michael

Anderson understood, your children need a strong, healthy, personal relationship with you. They need a direct connection to your heart that is maintained daily and weekly. They need you to make family your first priority after your personal relationship with God.

The word *benevolent* means "with a desire to do good or goodwill." It refers to doing good without seeking to make a profit. By now, you might be thinking, "Isn't this basic?" Yes. In fact, all of these primary needs are basic—balanced restraint, biblical resources, and healthy relationships. In fact, they are so basic, we've left them behind. We don't pray with our children. We don't spend time with them. We don't nurture and cherish them. We don't restrain them. And, as a result, we don't know them.

As we draw this book to a close, please understand that balanced restraint and biblical resources must find their resting place on the soft pillow of a healthy, heart-to-heart relationship between you and your child. It has been said that rules without relationships breed rebellion. Even so, you must spread your parenting efforts evenly. You must balance your restraint with relationship. You must give relational nurture equal time. Before we explore the solution, let's get a grip on the problem at hand.

Understanding the Problem

In most American homes, parents are consumed with providing toys, comforts, and fun to the point that they've stopped providing the most basic needs of the human heart—loving restraint, biblical training, and heart-level relationships. Our children have PlayStations and iPods but they don't have our hearts and we don't have theirs. Somewhere along the way, we have had a major disconnect when it comes to our family relationships.

This disconnect creates a devastating downward slide in the home. The less we know our family, the less we like them. The less we like them, the less time we spend at home. Thus, home becomes a pitstop—a place to sleep and refuel as fast as possible—so we can get back to what we really consider important. The most tragic result of this trend is that often our children will ultimately end up rejecting God. If their own parents, who claim to love and serve God, refuse to have a healthy relationship with them, why would they want a healthy relationship with God? Rejecting God becomes another link in the chain of rejecting the entire family.

Without healthy relationships, children grow up with no understanding of true love and purpose. They feel insignificant and end up pursuing false significance through sin and vice well into adulthood. Because the heart craves these good relationships, they end up chasing after false love and harmful relationships—like a starving refugee scavenging for food. The heart becomes so desperate for love that it will fall for just about any artificial substitute.

Ephesians 6:1–4 says, *"Children, obey your parents in the Lord: for this is right. Honour thy father and mother; (which is the first commandment with promise;) That it may be well with thee, and thou mayest live long on the earth. And, ye fathers, provoke not your children to wrath: but bring them up in the nurture and admonition of the Lord."* Here we are admonished to bring our children up in the nurture and admonition of the Lord. This requires connected relationships.

You may think your teenager doesn't desire to be close to you. But what you may be seeing is a heart so angry at the distance between you, it is choosing a path of greater distance! When teenagers flee to wrong friends and find every chance they can to get away from their parents, they are responding in anger to a relational distance that should never have existed in the first place.

You may think your younger son or daughter is doing just fine as you work all that extra overtime. He may appear to be all right with only occasional, minimal contact with you. Everything on the surface may seem to be normal, but in time, this lack of relationship—this lack of closeness—will have a devastating impact.

If you have experienced this relational disconnect in your home, you must respond immediately to fix the problem. Let's begin by seeing what a healthy relationship looks like.

A Profile of Healthy Home Relationships

Many parents are "first generation" Christians. In other words, they've never seen a good model of what a close family looks like! For others, we've drifted so far from God's design, that the model we're comparing to is only a distorted image of the original.

What do healthy home relationships look like from day to day? Here are a few thoughts.

1. Family members are glad to see each other. Are your kids glad to see you when you arrive home from work? Do they stop what they are doing to connect with you? In a healthy home, family members look forward to being together.

2. **Mealtime is a connection time.** Do you eat together as a family, or do family members eat spread out all over the house—watching television, studying, playing video games? Healthy families come together several times a week just to eat together. During that meal, a connection is shared. It's not an "eat and run" setting.

3. **Individual time together is a priority.** When is the last time you made a plan to spend individual time with each member of your family? Have you planned recent dates with your daughters? Have you taken your sons out for a few hours just to be together, doing something they enjoy? Healthy families spend one-on-one time together.

4. **Family time is a priority.** This involves having the whole family together to play a game, read a book, take a walk, or spend the day together. When is the last time your family spent the whole day together just being a family?

5. **Prayer and devotions are a part of family life.** Would your children think it strange if you pulled out a Bible and started reading it to them? If

so, there is a spiritual relationship disconnect in your home that must be reconnected. Spiritual growth should be a normal part of your weekly and daily family time.

6. Conversation goes beneath the surface. Healthy families talk about more than weather, grades, sports, and school. Healthy families share their hearts together. Teens who are close to their parents ask questions about life, the future, God, and decisions. Children who are close to their parents will share their emotions and hearts desires.

7. Time together is unrushed and frequent. Healthy families make time together a frequent occurrence.

8. Playing together is a priority. In healthy families, the children would rather spend the day with Mom and Dad than anyone else!

9. Conflict is resolved immediately. Close families don't go to sleep angry at one another. They don't have arguments and then just "forget about them." Close families resolve conflict. Parents apologize to kids and vice-versa. Reconciliation is a high and immediate priority, and life comes to a halt until relationships are made right.

10. Others are preferred consistently. Healthy families view family as a team. Each is pulling for the other, and all are working together for the good of the whole family. This interdependent spirit is quite a contrast to the world's model of an independent family.

Now, you may look at that list and feel that your family is "nowhere close!" If that's the case, don't become discouraged! Become encouraged that you have a great God who has the power to help you restore what has been lost. He can help you build what may never have been in place in your home. Don't look back in regret over what "hasn't been." Look forward in hope to what will be, and begin making godly changes today. Let's see how you can get started right now.

How To Reconnect the Hearts in Your Home

Reconnecting a family that has grown apart can at first be an uphill battle. Individual family members tend to "create their own turf." Drawing a family back together invades that turf and calls for a little resistance at first. Be prepared for this, and persist through it. God has called you to establish strong relationships with your family, and He will bless you as you press forward.

It takes only three basic elements to begin building close relationships at home. I encourage you to incorporate these actions as you strive to reconnect the hearts in your home.

Element #1—Time

Close families spend time together, and wise parents are constantly blocking off time for family and refusing to allow anyone or anything else to intervene. Amazingly, it seems that the older our children become, the less we think they need time with us. Exactly the opposite is true. The more they grow, the more they need time with you.

There is simply no short cut or quick fix to this problem. Time is the only real solution. No matter the condition of your relationship right now, time together will begin to heal it. No matter how much your child or teen resists spending time with you at first, deep in their heart they crave this time and need it more than they comprehend.

Imagine that a bank credits your account each morning with $86,400. No balance is carried over from day to day. Any balance is deleted each evening. What would you do if you knew that you would not use all your daily balance? Why, withdraw every penny, of course!

You have such a bank and so have I. The name of our bank is TIME. Every day we are credited with 86,400 seconds. Every night, what we have not used is debited from our account. TIME bank allows no overdraft; there is no going back for a second chance. TIME bank does not allow borrowing from tomorrow, and there are no leftovers. The clock ticks away, never waiting for sluggards to catch up, never waiting for what might have been; relentlessly, the clock ticks and ticks.

Friend, the clock is ticking. You are given a short amount of time to rear your children. Postponing time with your children is not merely putting it off. It is giving away time that can never be reclaimed. The next time you find yourself putting off time with your children, ask yourself, "Is this more important than being with my children?"

First Peter 3:7 says, *"Likewise, ye husbands, dwell with them according to knowledge, giving honour unto the wife, as unto the weaker vessel, and as being heirs together of the grace of life; that your prayers be not hindered.*" The word *dwell* means "to settle down in a fixed place." God intends for your family to have quantity, quality time together on a consistent basis.

There are several keys to making this "time" work. First, it must be consistent. One day a month is not enough. View this time with family the way you view feeding your body—it is a daily occurrence. You must have daily and weekly time with your kids to maintain that close connection to their hearts.

Second, it must be abundant. The average father spends less than five minutes a day talking to his children. Quantity time creates an environment where defenses can be let down and hearts can reconnect.

Third, it must be highly relational. Watching television or a movie is not relational. Talking, walking, and playing together is relational. If you are serious about establishing benevolent relationships in your home, be serious about creating relational time together.

Element #2—Transparent Communication

Transparency is a sincere openness to each other, and it must flow first from the parent. You must be honest about the condition of your relationship before it can be repaired. If there is a breach in your relationship, be transparent. Transparency involves confessing, apologizing, and seeking the forgiveness of your child. Transparency is sincerely asking, "How have I hurt you?" "What can I do to love you better?" (Without lashing out or defending self when the answer comes.) Transparency lets down defenses and communicates a desire to love at a heart level.

Transparency involves vulnerability. It means that you will become vulnerable to your own child if that's what it takes to heal the relationship and to keep it healthy. It means when the spirit of your child is closed to you, you will go to that child and sincerely seek restoration.

Transparency means you must openly admit when a relationship isn't right and seek God's help together in healing it.

God wants us to communicate openly and frequently with our kids. With one in four young people now indicating that they have never had a meaningful conversation with their father, is it any wonder that 76 percent of the 1,200 teens surveyed in *USA Today* actually want their parents to spend more time with them?

For instance, if I asked my child how his day was, I would expect him to say "Fine." But, if I asked my child what he did that day, I would expect a longer response. It might take extra effort to ask more intuitive questions, but the right questions will help you understand the heart of your child.

Learning to communicate effectively and transparently with your children is a lifelong journey. Every child is uniquely different. When parents make the effort and are concentrated on establishing and maintaining a relationship, the child will catch on and realize their parents desire a good, healthy relationship.

Element #3—Submission

Submission is giving yourself to meet the needs of another. Ephesians 5:21 says, *"Submitting yourselves one to another in the fear of God."* God desires for your home to be an environment where each family member is giving himself in service to the others. Parents should submit selflessly to the spiritual good of the children. Children should submit selflessly to honoring their parents. Siblings should submit selflessly to the well-being of the other. This is a beautiful picture of a Christian home—each member of the family willingly living for the good of one another.

Willing submission cannot be mandated. It must be demonstrated. It is better caught than taught. Your children will learn this as you exhibit it in your own life.

You will not believe how close the hearts of your family will become as you begin submitting yourselves one to another—beginning with Dad and Mom. Selfless love speaks loudly! Giving yourself to another person in humble, servant-hearted submission will do more to draw their heart to you than anything else.

When is the last time you gave your son or daughter the entire day with you? No young person could enjoy that kind of time without recognizing it as a gift. Your children know how busy you are. They know what you enjoy, and when you sacrifice something personal for their good, it speaks volumes!

In any close relationship, each person submits to the good of the other. The same will be true in your home. As you begin submitting one to another, living for the good of the others first, God will knit your hearts together in close relationship.

Conclusion

Three tools every Christian home must use effectively to reverse the trend of the disintegration of the American family:

Balanced Restraint
Biblical Resources
Benevolent Relationships

By now, you've discovered that healing your home is more about fixing the parents than it is about fixing the children! I hope you have received these thoughts with an open heart, and I pray that God has used them to stir within you a passion to recover the lost art of "family"!

The Apostle Paul wrote to the church at Philippi, reminding them of his testimony in their midst. He said, *"Those things, which ye have both learned, and received, and heard, and seen in me, do: and the God of peace shall be with you"* (Philippians 4:9).

Paul emphasized his example more than obedience to abstract principles. He stressed that they should do what they had learned, received, heard, and seen in him. In your home you must do the same. You must say to your child, "The things that you hear, learn, receive, and see in me—do." You must commit to living the right example in each of these areas before you can compel them to follow your example.

Are you parenting by example in these three areas? Do your children see your balanced restraint in your relationship with God? Do they see that you love biblical resources and obey God from the heart? Do they see you reaching out in self-sacrifice to establish loving relationships?

Hannah modeled a godly life of balanced restraint.

Pearl Harbor reminded us to put the right resources into action.

The testimony of Astronaut Michael Anderson reminded us that reaching for the stars is not nearly as important as relating closely with our children.

Now, it's your turn to fly. With God as your pilot, and His Word as your guide, may you rest in His strength, grow in His grace, and rely on His wisdom to safely land your family in the arms of Jesus Christ.

Other mini books available from Striving Together

These powerful little books make
perfect gifts of encouragement!

Done
by Cary Schmidt

Specifically created to be placed into the hands of an
unsaved person and a perfect gift for first-time church
visitors, this new mini book explains the Gospel in
crystal clear terms.

All Things through Christ
by Dr. Paul Chappell

Discover the ten words in Scripture that make
the difference for those who desire to live fully for
Jesus Christ.

Ten Principles for Biblical Living
by Dr. Don Sisk

Drawing from over fifty-two years of ministry experience
and a profound impact on world-wide missions, Dr. Don
Sisk shares ten biblical and practical principles that have
shaped his life and ministry. These principles will call
you to a renewed life of service for Jesus Christ and are
perfect for sharing with others as well.

www.strivingtogether.com
800.201.7748

For more information about our ministry visit the following websites:

www.strivingtogether.com
for helpful Christian resources

www.dailyintheword.org
for an encouraging word each day

www.lancasterbaptist.org
for information about Lancaster Baptist Church

www.wcbc.edu
for information about West Coast Baptist College